Clinical Pharmacokinetics and Therapeutic Drug Monitoring

By

Dr. Eswar Gupta Maddi

Professor

Sir C. R. Reddy College of Pharmaceutical Sciences, Eluru A.P., India

Dedicated

to my

Parents

About The Author

1. Dr. Eswar Gupta Maddi has done his B.Pharm at V.L. College of pharmacy, Raichur, Karnataka, during 1986 – 1990.

2. He later worked as a lecturer for Diploma in pharmacy inDr. Zakir Hussain College, Ibrahimpatnam, Krishna district, Andhra Pradesh.

3. In 1993, he qualified the all India GATE exam with 99.07 percentile.

4. He did his M.Pharmacy from Andhra University, Visakhapatnam, during the period 1993 to 1995. He secured a gold medal for standing first in pharmaceutical technology branch.

5. Later, he joined as a lecturer in K.V.S.R Siddhartha College of Pharmaceutical Sciences, Vijayawada, A.P., in the year 1995. He worked there till 2004.

6. In 2004, he joined ChalapathiInstitute of Pharmaceutical Sciences, Guntur, A.P., as Asst.

7. Professor. He was promoted there, as Professor in the year 2008. He continued as a professor till 2012.

8. In 2012, he joined Sir C.R.Reddy College of Pharmaceutical Sciences, Eluru, A.P., as professor in pharmaceutical technology department.

9. Till date he has a total teaching and research experience of22 years.

Learning to Read Correctly

1. First **understand** the topic / concept.

2. Prepare notes from **one standard text book**. Read the topic in text book, **close it** and write your notes in **your own language**. You can see the text book in the middle if you want.

3. Now learn your prepared notes. It will take around **2 to 3 hours** for one chapter for the first time.

4. When you try to **recollect** the lesson, the next day, **you forget** it. Hence **revision** is required. **Forgetting is a God's gift**, otherwise we would have been very sad remembering all the bad things in our life.

5. Revise the lesson **after one week**. Now you will take **2 hours** for learning it.

6. **Revise** after another week. It will take now **1 hour**.

7. On the exam day, you will take **less than 1 hour** for each chapter. You can complete eight chapters in 5 to 6 hours.

8. If you **start learning all eight chapters** before the exam day, it will take **16 to 24 hours** and you will get confused.

9. So, u should **not postpone** learning. Learn the chapter, **as soon as it is completed** in the class.

10. In case of chemistry, maths, etc. you have to practice the structures and equations by writing them repeatedly.

Positive Auto Suggestions

Input is equal to output. Example: If u see a comedy movie u laugh, if u see an emotional movie u may cry, if u see a violent movie u may become violent. So, input is equal to output.

If u start your day by reading the below positive auto suggestions, you will remain positive entire day and u will be successful in life.

By reading these auto suggestions daily once in the morning and once in the night, you are programming your brain to think and act positively in all situations.

1. I am an honest, cool, calm and relaxed person.

2. I am good in studies.

3. I always look for positive things in every person and every situation.

4. I will not run away from problems, I will solve them.

5. I am always with good and positive people.

6. I will always practice healthy habits.

7. I respect myself and others.

8. I always wish good for others.

9. I love my job and will work hard with dedication.

10. I will never postpone things.

11. I always do right things.

12. I give more than what I get to my family, organization and society.

13. I practice self-discipline and always finish what I start.

14. I take full responsibility for my thoughts and actions.

15. I am a courageous person.

16. I will improve daily.

17. I am always smiling.

18. I am happy with what I have.

19. I will always discuss, instead of arguing. (Argument is to find out who is right, discussion is to find out, what is right.)

20. I will walk daily for one hour.

21. I will take only healthy food.

22. I will meditate daily for 30 minutes.

23. I will always teach moral values to children.

24. I am healthy and always energetic.

25. I will take care of my parents with respect, love and affection.

For further details on positive thinking, please read the book,**"You Can Win" written by Mr. Shiv Khera.**It is a wonderful book that everyone should read. So far, 26 lakhs books have been sold in sixteen languages.

By following the principles of this book, you can achieve your goals and live happily. It describes the tools, you need for success.

This book will help you to create an action plan for rest of your life. The principles of this book are universal, you can apply in any situation, anywhere.

Another book worth reading is, **"How to win friends and Influence people"** by **Mr. Dale Carnegie**. It was first published in 1937 and is translated into all languages spoken in the world. This book will help you in maintaining a healthy relationship with everyone at work and family.

Unit NO	Contents	Page NO

Unit 1: Introduction to Clinicalpharmacokinetics

1.0: Introduction to clinical pharmacokinetics:

1. Pharmacokinetics deals with **speed** of ADME of drugs.

2. Application of pharmacokinetic principles in design of **dosage regimen** for an **individual** patient, is called clinical pharmacokinetics.

3. For example, the dosage regimen of a drug is **500 mg** every 6 hours.

4. If a patient has **50 % kidney failure**, dose is reduced by half to**250 mg** every 6 hours.

5. This dosage regimen will provide **optimum therapeutic efficacy** with minimum side effects.

6. Drugs like penicillin's, cephalosporin's, tetracyclineshave**broad therapeutic ranges**. The dose is fixed by the doctor depending on the severity of the infection. Fixing dosage regimen for individual patients is **not necessary.**

7. Individual dosage regimen is **required** for drugs with **narrow therapeutic range.**

8. Example: Digoxin, aminoglycosides, anti-asthmatics, anticonvulsants, have **narrow therapeutic index**. Dosage regimen should be

1

fixed for each individual patient. The dose should be adjusted, so that the plasma concentration of drug will be **between MEC** (minimum effective concentration) **and MSC** (maximum safe concentration).

9. **Monitoring plasma concentration** is useful only when there is a **correlation** between **plasma drug concentration and therapeutic effect**or adverse effects.

10. If there is no correlation between plasma concentration and therapeutic effect, other **pharmacodynamicparameters** must be used.

11. Example: In case of **warfarin, clotting time** is correlated with dose.

12. The therapeutic range published in books or research articles are **statistical average values**. They just provide **guidance** for fixing dose. Example: The therapeutic range for **theophylline** is**10 to 20 μg/ml**. Some patients show therapeutic response below 10 μg/ml, some patients have insomnia (side effect) below 20 μg/ml. So, doses should be adjusted for individual patients.

13. The therapeutic range of some potent drugsare given below.

14. Phenytoin: **10 to 20** micro gram/ml

15. Amikacin: **20 to 30** micro gram / ml.

16. Digoxin: **1 to 2**nano gram / ml.

17. In a new patient, the dosage regimen is first fixed basing on the patient's **body weight**andknown pharmacokinetic parameters of drug, patient's condition and patient's drug history.

18. The therapeutic drugmonitoring (TDM) departmenttake blood samples, from patients, analyze them and adjust the dose if necessary.

19. The new dosage regimen will provide **optimum therapeutic efficacy** with minimum side effects.

1.1: Functions of TDM (Therapeutic drug monitoring): The different functions of TDM are discussed below.

1: Selection of drug: Generally, the **doctor selects** the drug and dosage form. Nowadays, manydoctors**consult the clinical pharmacist**for**selection** of drug product and dosage regimen design. Therapeutic considerations, pharmacokinetic considerations and cost is considered by the clinical pharmacist in design of dosage regimen.

2: Dosage regimen design:

1. The objective of dosage regimen design is to achieve a **target concentration** at **receptor site**.
2. Dosage regimen is to be **fixed basing on** age, weight, disease condition (renal disease, hepatic disease, and cardiac failure), gender, nutritional status and genetic condition of patient.
3. Personal life style factors like **smoking, alcohol abuse and obesity**alsoalter pharmacokinetics of a drug.

3: Pharmacokinetics of the drug:

1. The pharmacokinetics data of a drug given in books or journals were obtained from **clinical studies in a small group of healthy volunteers**.
2. **Difference in study design**, patient population and data analysis may give **different values** for the same pharmacokinetic parameter.
3. So, it is advisable to take the **therapeutic window range** from the books or journals and

adjust the dosage regimenso that the plasma concentration of drug will be within this range.

4: Drug Dosage form:

1. A proper **dosage form and route of administration** is to be **selected** to achieve the necessary therapeutic effect.
2. If the drug concentration is to be maintained in a **narrow therapeutic range**, a **loading dose** followed by **I.V infusion or long acting oral product** can be given.

5: Patient compliance:

1. **Cost of the medication, complicated instructions, multiple daily doses**, side effects affect patient compliance.
2. **Life style and needs of the patient** should be considered while designing a dosage regimen.
3. Instead of many single doses per day, a **sustained release product** can be given to the patient.

6: Evaluation of patient's response:

1. After the initial dosage regimen, the physician should **evaluate the clinical response of the patient.**
2. If the patient is **not responding**, then the dosage regimen should be readjusted.
3. If necessary, **blood samples**must be taken and **analyzed** for drug concentration. Then a new dosage regimen is to be designed.

7: Measurement of concentration of drug in blood serum:

1. Blood samples are to be taken **only if the patient's response** is related to plasma drug concentration.
2. A **single plasma concentration** may not give the necessary information in multiple dosage regimen.
3. A **blood sample** taken in the **post distributive phase** correlates well with tissue concentration.
4. Blood samples taken after **three or four half lives** in a multiple dosage regimen will give the **steady state plasma concentration**.

5. The physician should consider the **cost of analysis, discomfort to patient** before going for blood samples.
6. Common **drugs monitored** in hospitals are given below.
7. Amikacin, gentamycin, tobramycin, cocaine, carbamazepine, opiates, digoxin, phenobarbital, phenytoin, digitoxin, barbiturates, theophylline, paracetamol, etc.

8: Pharmacokinetic evaluation:

1. The labs generally give the plasma **concentration of total drug** (protein bound + free drug).
2. The pharmacokinetic scientist should **compare** it with the values given in the books or journals.
3. The patient plasma concentration may be **more or less or same** as the values given in the books or journals.
4. The scientist should **interpret this data** after considering the patient's disease condition.
5. **High plasma creatinine** concentration and **blood urea nitrogen** (BUN) may indicate the kidney is not functioning properly.

7

6. The **possible reasons for lowerdrug concentration in blood** are given below

a) Patient **not taking** medicines regularly

b) **Error** in dosage regimen

c) **Poor bioavailability** of tablet

d) **Rapid elimination** of drug by patient

e) **Fast metabolism** of drug by patient

f) **Timing** of blood sample

g) Patient **renal and hepatic function improving**

h) **Drug drug interactions**

7. The **possible reasons for higherplasma drug concentration** are...

a) Patient **not taking** medicines regularly

b) **Error** in dosage regimen

c) **Rapid bioavailability** of tablet

d) **Slow elimination / metabolism** of drug by patient

e) **Timing** of blood sample

f) **Drug drug interactions**

9: Dosage adjustment:

1. From the plasma drug concentration data and patient observation, a **new dosage regimen is designed**. The data **may not be sufficient** to calculate all the pharmacokinetic parameters,

8

but the scientist must be able to **design the regimen** using the available data and population pharmacokinetic parameters available from the books.

2. In many cases, the patient condition may **improve or deteriorate**.Example: After a congestive cardiac failure, **the patient may improve** on treatment. Renal blood flow increases and elimination of drug increases. **In such cases, again the dosage regimen** is to be modified.

3. For some drugs,**acute pharmacological response** can be monitored after altering dosage regimen. Example: Blood pressure change can be monitored with dosage regimen change.

4. The patient may not respond to therapy due to other reasons, like missing doses, **not following instructions to take medicine after food**, or may be on low sodium diet. In such cases, the patient should be given simple instructions.

5. Hence by TDM, we can provide the patient **optimum therapeutic efficacy**with minimum side effects.

Unit 2: Design of Dosage Regimens

2.0:Introduction:

1. There are **several methods to adjust** the dosage regimen in a patient.

2. The **initial dose** is fixed basing on the population pharmacokinetic parameters available in books or journals.

3. The patient is then **monitored for therapeutic response** / plasma drug levels and if necessary dosage regimen is modified.

4. **Many software** are available for dose calculations of drugs with narrow therapeutic index. Example: **Data kinetics, Abbott base pharmacokinetic system.** Software makes calculations and dose adjustments easy.

2.1:Nomograms and Tabulations in designing dosage regimen:

1. Kidneys and liver are **the two major organs** for drug elimination. When kidneys or livers are affected, it is necessary to adjust the dose of drugs.

2. **Nomograms are graphs** which can be used to calculate the dose of a drug for a patient basing on his age, weight, and diseased state.

3. **Creatinine clearance**is used to determine the extent of kidney function.

4. A simple nomogram is shown below. It can be **used in patients with reduced renal function**.

5. The dosage adjustment factor can be used to adjust the maintenance dose and dosing interval.

6. The nomogram is constructed basing on the equation $Q = 1 - f(1-K)$

7. Q = Dosage adjustment factor,

8. f = fraction of drug eliminated by kidney,

9. K = extent of kidney function = creatinine clearance of patient / 130.

10. Example: Dose of a drug is 500 mg, given every 6 hours, fraction eliminated by kidneys is 0.2, creatinine clearance is 65 ml/min, calculate the new dose.

   $Q = 1 - 0.2 (1 - 0.5) = 1 - 0.2 (0.5) = 1 - 0.1 = 0.9$

11. Dose = Q x 500 g = 0.9 x 500 = 450 mg.**Do not change dosing interval here.**

12. New dosing interval =Dosing interval in normal person / Q
   = 6/0.9 = 6.66 hours.

13. So, give the patient 500 mg every 6.6 hours.

14. **If dosing interval is changed, dose should not be adjusted**.

15. The **values of 'f'** can be obtained from books and journals. Example: Values of 'f' for **tetracycline is 0.6 and trimethoprim is 0.7.**

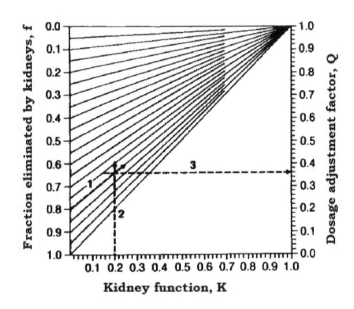

16. **If we know f and k,** we can calculate Q from the above graph.

17. **Tabulations (Tables) are provided by manufacturers**for dosage adjustments in patients. It contains the dose to be given for each class of patients. An example is given below for theophylline.

Dose of Theophylline

S.NO	Age in years	Dose in mg/kg/day
1	6 to 9	24
2	9 to 12	20
3	12 to 16	18
4	Greater than 16	13

2.2:Conversion from intravenous to oral dosing:

1. When the physician wants to stop the IV infusion, and convert to oral route of administration, it is **better to use controlled release products.** Itwill maintain the plasma concentration of drug in therapeutic range.

2. Oral controlled release therapy should be **started immediately** when the IV therapy is stopped.

3. The following **equation** can be used to calculate the dose and dosing interval for the oral product.

13

4. **Dose / hour = Steady state concentration X clearance / F**

5. F = Bio availability factor

6. Example: Calculate the dose of a drug to maintain a steady state blood concentration of 2 mg/L. The total clearance of the drug is 6 L/hr. Thebioavailability factor of the oral product is 0.8.

7. Dose/hour = 2 x 6 /0.8 = 15 mg / hr.

8. So, the dose for one day = 15 x 24 = 360 mg/ day.

9. Give the patient a controlled release product having 180 mg, every 12 hours. It will release 15 mg / hr for 12 hours.

10. In another method, the IV infusion rate is used for calculating the dose and dosing interval.

11. Example: Drug is given by IV infusion at the rate of 20 mg/hour. Calculate the oral dose and dosing interval.

12. The total daily dose is 20 x 24 = 480 mg.

13. So, select a controlled release product with 240 mg. It is to be taken two times a day. It will release the drug at a controlled rate of 20 mg/hour.

2.3: Determination of dose and dosing intervals:

1. The dose and dosing interval can be calculated from the **steady state plasma concentration** to be maintained.

2. The steady state concentration of drug in blood should be within the **therapeutic range**.

3. The therapeutic range for drugs can be found in books and journals.

4. First calculate the dosing interval using the **Cssmax and Cssmin**.

5. $Cssmax/Cssmin = 1 / e^{-K\tau}$

6. 'K' is the elimination rate constant of the drug and 'τ' (tau) is the dosing interval.

7. 'e' is a mathematical constant having a value of 2.718

8. The below equation gives the **relation between** steady state concentration, dose and dosing interval.

9. **Css = (1.44) (D) $(t_{1/2})$ (F) / (V_d) (dosing interval)**

10. Using the above equations, we can calculate the dose and dosing interval to maintain the desired steady state concentration.

2.4:Drug dosing in pediatrics:

1. The pharmacokinetics of drugs is different in **new born infants**(0 to 28 days), **infant** (28 days to 23 months),**young child** (2 to 5 years), **older child** (6 to 11 years), **adolescent** (12 to 18 years) and **adult**(above 18 years).

2. Unfortunately, the pharmacokinetics and pharmacodynamics of drugs is **not well known** in children below 12 years.

3. Variation in body composition and **maturity of liver and kidney function** is responsible for differences in pharmacokinetics of drugs.

4. New born infants (0 to 4 weeks) handle drugs differently when compared with mature infants (2 to 23 months age). Hence, drugs are to be given more carefully in new born infants.

5. Generally, it takes **three week time** for complete hepatic function to be attained.

6. New born show only **30 to 50 % of activity** in renal function when compared with adults. Hence, drugs being majorly eliminated by kidneys will have more half-life in new born.

7. Example: **Half-life of penicillin is 3.2 hours** in neonates (0 to 7 days old) and 0.5 hours in adults. The dose is 4 mg/kg body weight,

every4 hours, calculate the dose and dosing interval for a neonate having 3 kg weight.

8. Dosing interval can be calculated using the below formula.

9. Dosing interval of adults / Dosing interval of infant = 0.5/3.2

10. Dosing interval of infant = 3.2 x 4 /0.5 = 25.6 hours.

11. Dose is 3 x 4 = 12 mg. So, give the neonate, 12 mg penicillin every 24 hours.

12. Other methods of dosage adjustments are made on age, weight and body surface area. The **Young's formula and Clark's formula** for dosage calculation do not take into account the renal clearance of drugs.

2.5:Drug dosing in elderly patients:

1. Elders are classified as **young old** (65 to 75), **old** (75 to 85), and **old old** (greater than 85).

2. Renal plasma flow, glomerular filtration, cardiac output and breathing capacity can decrease from **10 to 30 %** in elders when compared with 30 years age people.

3. The **quantity and quality of drug receptors** may change with age.

4. Due to physiological changes, ADME gets altered in elders.

5. Blood flow to GIT gets reduced, GI motility decreases, increase in GI pH, and absorption of drugs decrease.

6. **Achlorhydria** is increased gastric pH. Weak basic drugs may fail to dissolve in the stomach due to achlorhydria in elders.

7. **Protein content** decreases with age, protein binding is less and free drug concentration available for distribution is more.

8. Renal plasma flow,glomerular filtration, decrease from 10 to 30 % in elders when compared with 30 years age people. As a result renal clearance of drugs decreases.

9. **Enzymes activity** in drug metabolism decreases with age and this reduces hepatic clearance of drugs.

10. In view of all these changes, the drug dosage regimen should be altered in elders.

11. Elders may have many diseases and may be on **multi drug therapy**, which may lead to drug interactions.

12. Increased adverse reactions and toxicity may also be due to poor patient compliance in elders.

13. Example: An aminoglycoside has a dose of 500 mgevery 12 hours. Calculate the dose for an elder of 75 years. Half-life in adults is 100 minutes and in elders is 300 minutes.

14. Answer: There is **good correlation between creatinine clearance** and half-life of drug.

15. $t_{1/2}$ in adult / $t_{1/2}$ in elder = τ in adult / τ in elders

16. 100 / 300 = 12 / τ in elders

17. τ in elders = 12 x 300 / 100 = 36 hours.

18. So, in elders give the same 500 mg dose every 36 hours.

19. The clearance of lithium in 25 year old people is 40 ml/minute, whereas in elders of 65 years it was found to be 8 ml/minute. Calculate the dose reduction in a patient with 65 years.

20. Answer: Dose reduction = 100 x Cl in elders/ Cl in 25 years

21. Dose reduction = 100 x 8 / 40 = 20 %. Reduce dose by 20 % for elders.

22. Dose in elders / dose in young = Cl in elders / Cl in young.

2.6:Dosing in obese patients:

1. A person is considered obese, if the weight is **greater by 20 %** than the ideal weight.

2. Obesity is defined by **body mass index**. (BMI).

3. **BMI = Body weight in kg/ (height in cm)^2**

4. The below table gives the different classes basing on BMI.

S.NO	BMI	Description
1	Less than 18.5	Under weight.
2	18.5 to 24.9	Normal weight.
3	25 – 29.9	Over weight.
4	30 – 39.9	Obese.
5	More than 40	Extreme obesity.

5. The obese patient has **greater fat tissue** than muscle tissue. Fat tissue has less water when compared to muscle tissue. This affects the distribution of drugs.

6. Example: Antipyrine Vd in obese patient was found to be 0.46 L/kg, where as in an ideal body weight person it was 0.62 L/kg.

7. Drug distribution gets altered due to **partitioning of drugs** between fat and aqueous environments. Example: Drugs such as digoxin

and gentamycin are polar and tend to distribute into aqueous compartments. If gentamycin dose is adjusted basing on body weight, it distributes to **extra cellular fluids** and toxic reactions may occur. Hence, its dose is to be adjusted basing on ideal body weight.

8. Lean body weight is estimated using the below equation and dose is adjusted basing on lean body weight.

9. LBW Men = 50 Kg + 2.3 Kg for each inch over 5 feet.

10. LBW Women = 45.5 kg + 2.3 Kg for each inch over 5 feet.

11. Example: The dose of a drug is 15 mg/kg, calculate the dose for an obese patient of height 5 feet eight inches.

12. LBW = 50 + (2.3 x 8) =68.4 kg.

13. Dose = 15 x 68.4 = 1028 mg.

14. **Lipophillic drugs** have larger **Vd** when compared with hydrophilic drugs. Hence effect of obesity on specific drugs must be considered for accurate dosing strategy.

15. In obese persons, **fatty infiltration** of liver affects drug metabolism.

16. Cardiovascular changes in obese persons affect renal flow and renal clearance. Hence dose

should be adjusted basing on body weight and patent condition.

Practice problems:

1. For a drug, the therapeutic range is 20 mg/L to 5 mg/L, calculate the dose and dosing interval. The elimination rate constant is 0.1/ hour. (Ans = 13.86 hours)

2. For the above drug, calculate the dose to maintain a steady state concentration of 10 mg/L. It has a half-life of 6.93 hours, a Vd of 10 L and bio availability of 0.8. (Ans = 175 mg)

3. Example: A drug dosage regimen is 500 mg every 6 hours. It has a half-life of 4 hours, a Vd of 10 L and bio availability of 0.8. Calculate the steady state concentration.

4. Css = 1.44 x 500 x 4 x 0.8 / 10 x 6 = 38.4 mg/L.

5. For the above drug, we can decrease the steady state concentration by **decreasing dose or by increasing dosing interval**.

6. Example: If we want to have a steady state concentration of19.2 mg / L for above drug, calculate the new dosing interval, dose is not to be changed.

7. Example: If we want to have a steady state concentration of19.2 mg / L for above drug, calculate the new dose, dosing interval is not to be changed.

Unit 3: Pharmacokinetics of Drug Interactions

3.1:Pharmacokinetic drug interactions:

1. Many patients will be on **multi drug therapy**.

2. When one drug **alters the action** of other drug it is called drug interaction.

3. In hospitalized patients, around **eight to twelve** drugs are used on an average.

4. Some drug interactions produce adverse effects.

5. Some drug interactions are **intentional** to produce therapeutic benefits to the patient.

6. Drug interactions types: Drug – drug interaction, food - drug interaction, drug – chemical (alcohol, smoking) interaction.

7. **Software is available** for screening of potential drug – drug interactions. However, the pharmacist must decide the impact of this interaction on the patient.

8. Drugs with interaction **should be avoided** or can be given at different time intervals to minimize the interaction.

9. If the half-life of a drug changes due to drug interaction, alter the dose or dosing interval.

10. Example: **Antacids** reduce bioavailability of antibiotics.

11. **Laxatives** increase GI motility and may reduce bioavailability of drug products.

12. **Anti cholinergic drugs** reduce GI motility, reduces gastric emptying of paracetamol and delays absorption from intestine.

13. Antacids reduce pH of stomach, and reduces dissolution of ketoconazole.

14. **Phenyl butazone** displaces warfarin from protein binding.

15. **Smoking** increases metabolism of theophylline.

16. **Phenobarbitone** increases metabolism of warfarin.

17. Verapamil inhibits **biliary excretion** of digoxin.

18. **Probencid** reduces renal clearance of penicillins.

19. Antacids make the **urine alkaline** and reduces renal excretion of basic drugs.

20. **Grapes reduce metabolism** of terfanidine and cyclosporine.

3.2:Inhibition of Drug metabolism:

1. When **one drug inhibits the metabolism** of another drug it is called inhibition of drug metabolism.

2. **Fluvoxamine** increases the half-lifeof diazepam by two times. So, double the dosing interval or reduce the dose by half.

3. **Quinidine** inhibits the metabolism of nifedipine and other calcium channel blockers. The reason for this is, both the drugs are metabolized by the same **cytochrome P 450 enzymes**. The half-life of nifidepine is increased by 40 %.

4. **Cimetidine** reduces metabolism of theophylline and the half-life may increase by 20 to 40 %. Elevated theophylline concentration may lead to nausea, vomiting, and even seizures.

5. **Interferon** reduces metabolism of theophylline and half-life is increased by 50 % from 8 to 12 hours.

6. **Cimetidine** reduces the microsomal enzyme oxidation of diazepam. As a result AUC increases, Cmax increases, tmax decreases, elimination rate constant and renal clearance decreases.

3.3:Induction of drug metabolism:

1. Cytochrome P 450 enzymes metabolize many drugs by oxidation.

2. Certain drugs like barbiturates **stimulate the production** of these hepatic enzymes. As a result metabolism of other drugs increases. This is called enzyme induction.

3. Example: **Barbiturates** increase the metabolism of warfarin(anti coagulant). So, warfarin dose is increased to compensate for this effect.

4. When**phenobarbitone** is stopped, warfarin dose should be readjusted to the original dose, otherwise severe hemorrhagic episodes may occur.

5. Other drugs that induce metabolism are **rifampicin, carbamazepine, phenytoin, valproic acid**. They reduce the half-life of other drugs.

6. Example: Phenobarbital reduces dexamethasone levels in asthamatic patients.

3.4:Inhibition of Biliary Excretion:

1. Bile juice is produced by liver and is **stored in gall bladder**.

2. It is secreted into the duodenum for digestion of fats. The bile flow rate is **0.5 to 1 ml per minute**. 90 % of the bile acids are reabsorbed from the intestine and is transported back to the liver for re secretion.

3. Drugs and their metabolites enter from the plasma to bile juice through hepatocytes (liver cells). This bile juice carries the drug and secretes in duodenum. Thus the drug comes out along with fecal matter. Some of the drug is again reabsorbed from intestine into blood and goes back to the liver. Again it is excreted by bile juice. This cycling of drugs is calledentero hepatic cycling of drugs.

4. Entero hepatic cycling is shown below.

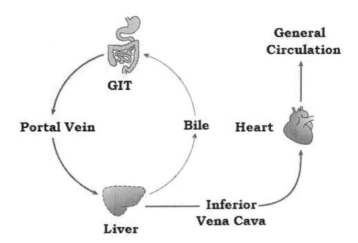

5. Sometimes one drug may inhibit the biliary clearance of other drugs. Example: **Verapamil reduced the biliary clearance of digoxin** in cardiac patients. Digoxin blood levels increased by 44 % in presence of verapamil. Hence dose of digoxin is to be adjusted.

Unit 4: Therapeutic Drug Monitoring

4.1:Introduction and objectives of TDM:

1. Therapeutic drug monitoring (TDM) is **measurement** of drug concentration in patient's blood at specific time intervals. Basing on this information, the dosage regimen is adjusted to maintain the drug concentration in the **therapeutic range**. As a result, treatment will be effective with minimal side effects.

2. TDM is required for drugs with **narrow therapeutic range**anddrugs with **pharmacokinetic variability** from person to person. Example: Digoxin, amino glycosides, anti arrhythmics, anti-asthmatics, anticonvulsants, require design of dosage regimen for each individual patient. The plasma concentration of drug should be between MEC (minimum effective concentration) and MSC (maximum safe concentration).

3. TDM is not necessary for drugs having **broad therapeutic range**. Example: Drugs like penicillins, cephalosporins, tetracyclines have broad safe dose ranges. The dose is fixed by the doctor depending on the severity of the infection.

4. TDM is useful only when there is a **correlation** between, dose, plasma concentration and therapeutic effect / adverse effects.
5. If there is **no correlation** between plasma concentration and therapeutic effect / adverse effects, other **pharmacodynamics parameters** must be used.
6. Example: In case of warfarin, clotting time is correlated with dose.
7. TDM team consists of **physicians, scientists, nurses and pharmacist**.
8. TDM begins when the drug is first prescribed basing on his age, weight, disease condition, etc.
9. TDM removes the trial and error approach for fixing a dosage regimen.

4.2: Individualization of drug dosage regimen: Dosage regimen should be fixed basing on the patient's age, weight, disease condition etc.

4.2.1 Dosage regimen adjustment due to genetics: See unit 7.

4.2.2 Drug dosing in pediatrics:See 2.4

4.2.3 Drug dosing in elderly patients: See 2.5

4.2.4 Dosing in obese patients: See 2.6

4.2.5: Dosage regimen in case of interacting drugs: See 3.1, 3.2, 3.3

4.2.6: Dosage regimen design in disease states: See 5.1

4.3: Indications for TDM: TDM is necessary in the following cases.

1. Therapeutic drug monitoring (TDM) is **measurement of drug** concentration in patient's blood at specific time intervals. Basing on this information, the **dosage regimen is adjusted** to maintain the drug concentration in the therapeutic range. As a result, treatment will be effective with minimal side effects.

2. TDM is required for drugs with narrow therapeutic range.Example: Digoxin, amino glycosides, anti arrhythmics, anti-asthmatics, anticonvulsants, require design of dosage regimen for each individual patient. The plasma concentration of drug should be between **MEC** (minimum effective concentration) and **MSC** (maximum safe concentration).

3. TDM is required for drugs having **pharmacokinetic variability** from person to person.

31

4. TDM is required when a drug follows **mixed order kinetics** in the body. Example: **Phenytoin** metabolism in liver follows mixed order kinetics. At **low doses** it is metabolized according to **first order** kinetics. At **high doses**, liver enzymes get saturated and metabolism follows **zero order** kinetics. As a result, concentration of drug is more in the body and toxic effects may occur. A small increase in dose may increase the therapeutic effects and adverse effects significantly. When the dose of phenytoin is increased from 300 mg/day to 450 mg/day, the steady state plasma concentration is increased by 10 times. This causes severe side effects.

5. TDM is required in **hepatic and renal diseases**. When drug clearance is reduced due to renal disease or hepatic dose, adjust dose and dosing interval.

6. TDM is required in **multiple drug therapy** and if drug interactions are present.

7. TDM is required if we have a doubt about **patient compliance**.

8. Drug assays are costly and TDM should be done if it is really necessary.

9. To assess loading dose and maintenance dose in long term therapy, TDM is required. Example: Phenytoin.

4.4: Protocol for TDM: The protocol for TDM study is given below.

1. Title of study:
2. Name of investigator:
3. Place of study:
4. Patient recruitment place:
5. Need for TDM study:
6. Objective for TDM study:
7. Criteria for selection of patient:
8. Patient history:
9. With drawl time of blood sample and storage:
10. Instrument used for analysis of drug concentration in blood / clinical parameters.
11. Report preparation.
12. Clinical interpretation.

4.5: Pharmacokinetic and Pharmacodynamic correlation in drug therapy:

1. Pharmacokinetics deals with speed of ADME of drugs.

2. Pharmacodynamics deals with concentration of drug at site of action or receptor and therapeutic effect / toxic effect.

3. It is difficult to measure concentration of drug at site of action or receptor, hence **blood /saliva/urine** concentration is measured and correlated with therapeutic effect.

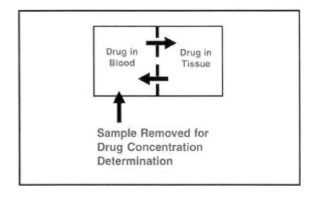

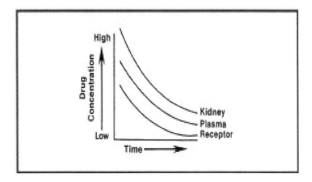

4. There is a direct relationship between drug concentration in blood and at site of action.

Hence we can **correlate**blood concentration of drug and therapeutic effect / adverse effects.

5. TDM is useful only if there is correlation between plasma concentration and therapeutic effect / adverse effects.

6. The relation with plasma concentration and therapeutic effect is given in the below graph. As, plasma concentration increases, therapeutic effect increases. **After certain concentration, therapeutic effect does not increases any further.**

7. For some drugs, the **effectiveness decreases with continuous use**. This may be due to increased metabolism of the drug or the receptors loosing sensitivity. Example: **Opiates** are used as pain killers. On repeated usage large doses and plasma concentrations are required to produce the same effect. This can be seen in the below graph.

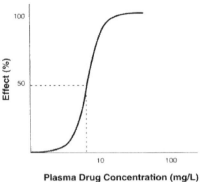

Plasma Drug Concentration (mg/L)

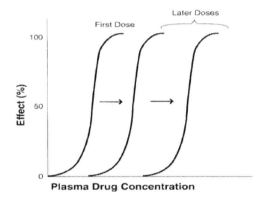

First Dose

Later Doses

Plasma Drug Concentration

8. If there is no correlation between plasma concentration and therapeutic effect / adverse effects, other pharmacodynamics parameters must be used.

9. Example: In case of warfarin, **clotting time** is correlated with dose.

10. Example: In case of anti-asthmatic drug albuterol, the product is given by a metered dose inhaler and is correlated with forced expiratory volume of the patient as a measure of drug efficacy.

TDM of drugs used in cardiovascular studies:
TDM of procainamide:

1. Procainamide is an anti-arrhythmic drug.
2. It is used orally in **prophylactic** treatment of arrhythmias.
3. It has a short half-life**(2.5 to 5 hours)** and a narrow therapeutic range of (4 to 8 mcg/ml). In some patients higher concentrations are effective.
4. Toxic effects are not seen up to**12 mcg/ml**. They are observed when the concentration in blood exceeds**16 mcg/ml**. Toxic effects include marked hypotension, ventricular arrhythmia and cardiac arrest.
5. Blood samples for monitoring are taken after **24 hours** after starting oral therapy. Steady state concentrations will be achieved after 24 hours. In case of renal disease patient **wait for 2 days for steady state** to be reached.

6. Two blood samples are taken. One is taken at the end of dosing interval and another is taken, 2 hours after administration. This gives the peak plasma concentration.

7. 40 to 60 % of drug is eliminated in urine. IV dose and oral dose should be reduced in patients with renal disease.

8. **N – Acetyl procainamide** is the main metabolite of procainamide. It also has therapeutic and toxic effects.

9. Some patients metabolize procainamide to a greater extent and NAP level is more in blood. **NAP also has antiarrhythmicaction**.This is the reason why some persons show good therapeutic effect with even low procainamide blood levels.

TDM of Quinidine:

1. Quinidineis an anti-arrhythmic drug.

2. It is used orally in prophylactic treatment and treatment of arrhythmias.

3. It has a half-life**(6 to 7 hours)** and a narrow therapeutic range(3 to 8 mcg/ml).

4. Toxic effects are observed when the concentration in blood exceeds 8 mcg/ml. Toxic effects include **reentrant arrhythmia** that can lead to heart blocks.

5. Blood samples for monitoring are taken after 12 hours after starting oral therapy.

6. Protein binding is **70 to 80 %.**

7. 80 % of the drug is metabolized in liver. The remaining is excreted unchanged in urine.

8. Intersubject variability in bioavailability is very significant and doses of 400 to 1200 mg/day is required to achieve therapeutic concentration range.

9. **Cimetidine and ketoconazole** inhibits the metabolism of quinidine.

10. **Phenytoin and rifampicin** enhances the metabolism of quinidine.

Prepare TDM notes for lidocaine, gentamicin, amikacin, carbamazepine, phenobarbital, phenytoin, and drugs used in organ transplantations. Use the proforma given in the next page to collect the TDM.

S.NO	TDM OF
1	Use
2	$t_{1/2}$
3	Therapeutic range
4	Toxic concentration
5	Toxic effects
6	IV dose
7	Oral Dose
8	Oral bioavailability
9	Oral bioavailability increased by
10	Oral bioavailability decreased by
11	% of metabolism
12	Metabolism induced by
13	Metabolism inhibited by
14	% protein binding
15	Protein binding increased by
16	Protein binding decreased by
17	Renal elimination %
18	Renal elimination increased by
19	Renal elimination decreased by
20	Blood sampling time intervals
21	Other information

Unit 5: Dosage Adjustment in Renal and Hepatic Disease

5.1:Renal impairment:

1. Kidney is responsible for **fluid balance, electrolyte balance, removal of drugs** and their metabolites from the body.

2. When kidney function decreases due to any reason, it is called renal impairment.

3. **Disease or injury or drug intoxication** is responsible for renal impairment.

4. Drug pharmacokinetics (Ke, t1/2) change with renal impairment.

5. Acute disease or major injury to kidney may cause **uremia**, GFR decreases and body fluids and **nitrogenous products** get accumulated in the body.

6. Uremia (High levels of urea in blood).

7. Uremia reduces **glomerular filtration** / active secretion of drugs. This increases the biological half-life of drugs in the body.

8. Dosage adjustments should be made in uremic patients.

9. Hypertension, diabetes, nephritis, and certain drugs (aminoglycosides, phenacetin, and heavy metals) may cause kidney failure.

5.2: Pharmacokinetic considerations:

1. In uremic patients, bio-availability, Vd and clearance of drugs get altered.

2. In severe uremia, G.I motility and pH of GIT changes. As a result, oral bio-availability of drugs changes.

3. Mesenteric blood flow to GIT may also be altered. As a resultbioavailability of drugs decreases.

4. The Vd of a drug depends on protein binding and **total body water**.

5. Protein binding of weak acidic drugs decrease in uremia patients. Protein binding of weak basic drugs does not change.

6. If **protein binding is reduced** free drug concentration increases.

7. Protein binding may be further reduced as a result of accumulation of metabolites and fatty acids, **urea in blood** may compete with the drug for protein binding.

8. Total body clearance of drugs decreases due to reduced GFR and reduced tubular secretion of drugs.

9. Dosage regimen adjustment is made on the basis of **remaining renal function** and total body clearance of drug.

10. A complete pharmacokinetic analysis of drug in the uremic patient is not possible, because**uremic condition is not stable** and may change too rapidly for pharmacokinetic analysis.

11. Dosing guidelines in uremic patients can be found in **Physicians' Desk reference book** and research literature.

5.3: General approach for dosage adjustment in Uremic patient / Renal disease:

1. There are several approaches to **adjust** the dosage in uremic patients.

2. The blood concentration should be maintained in the therapeutic range as for a normal person. This can be done by **reducing the dose or by increasing the dosing interval** in uremic patient.

3. The design of dosage regimen will be based on the changed elimination pharmacokinetics of the drug. Generally the **half-life of the drug and Vd** increases in severe uremic patients.

4. In less severe cases, there will be no edema or change in Vd. In such cases, dose adjustment can be made basing on the **drug clearance** from the body.

5. Generally dosage adjustment is made using **drug clearance values** and elimination half-life values.

6. This can be done by determining the **renal clearance** of the drug in uremic patient.

7. Now we have to find the ratio of renal clearance of drug in uremic patient and ordinary person.

8. Fraction of kidney function = **Cl_U/ Cl_N**

9. Cl_U = Clearence in uremic patient.

10. Cl_N = Clearence in normal person.

11. **Dose in uremic patient (D_U) = Fraction of kidney function x (D_N)**

12. Example: The normal renal clearance of a drug is 200 ml/minute and in a uremic patient is 50 ml/minute. The normal dose is 400 mg every six hours. Find out the dose for the uremic patient.

13. Fraction of kidney function = 50/200 = 0.25

14. D_U = 0.25 x 400 = 100 mg every six hours.

15. Oral dose or IV dose or IV infusion has to be adjusted in the same manner. Do not change dosing interval.

5.4: Dosage adjustment based on changes in elimination rate constant:

1. The **elimination rate constant decreases** in uremic patients.
2. Dosage regimen can be changed by reducing dose without altering dosing interval or by altering dosing interval without adjusting the dose.
3. In case of narrow therapeutic range drugs, **reduce dose** keeping dosing interval constant.
4. Determine the ratio K_U / K_N. Multiply this with the normal dose, we will get the dose for uremic patient. Dosing interval is same as that for normal person.
5. Certain assumptions are made while determining the renal elimination rate constant in uremic patients.
6. The renal elimination rate constant decreases **linearly** with kidney function. If kidney function decreases by half, the renal elimination rate constant also decreases by half.

7. The non-renal routes of elimination (liver metabolism, salivary excretion, biliary excretion etc.) remain unchanged.

8. Changes in renal clearance of drugs is reflected by changes in **creatinine clearance.**

9. The overall elimination rate constant depends on the renal and all non renal excretion.

10. $K_U = K_{nr} + K_{rU}$

11. K_U = Elimination rate constant in uremic patient.

12. K_{nr} = Non renal elimination rate constant in normal person.

13. K_{rU} = Renal elimination rate constant in uremic patient = Cl_u/Vd.

14.   Creatinine clearance of patient is used to measure renal function in uremic patient.

5.6: Dosage adjustment in Uremic patients using Nomograms:

1. Dose adjustments should be done basing on the pharmacokinetic and pharmacodynamic changes of drug in uremic patients.

2. The **loading dose** is based on the volume of distribution of the patient. Generally, it is assumed that the volume of distribution is not significantly different. The loading dose is same as for persons with normal renal function.

46

3. The **maintenance dose** is based on the renal clearance of the drug. The extent of kidney function is estimated by creatinine clearance.

4. After calculating the creatinine clearance, the maintenance dose or dosing interval or both are changed.

5. Nomograms (charts) are available for adjustments of dose basing on renal clearance and pharmacokinetics of drugs.

6. Nomograms are developed for **each drug** using the creatinine clearance value and assuming that the non-renal clearance of drug is not altered in the uremic patient.

7. A simple nomogram is shown below. The dosage adjustment factor can be used to adjust the maintenance dose and dosing interval.

8. The nomogram is constructed basing on the equation $Q = 1 - f(1-K)$

9. Q = Dosage adjustment factor

10. f = fraction of drug eliminated by kidney

11. K = extent of kidney function = creatinine clearance of patient / 130.

12. Example: Dose of a drug is 500 mg, every 6 hours, fraction eliminated by kidneys is 0.2, creatinine clearance is 65, calculate the dose.

$Q = 1 - 0.2 (1 - 0.5) = 1 - 0.2 (0.5) = 1 - 0.1 = 0.9$

13. Dose = Q x 500 g = 0.9 x 500 = 450 mg. Do not change dosing interval here.

14. New dosing interval =Dosing interval in normal person / Q
    = 6/0.9 = 6.66 hours.

    If dosing interval is changed, dose should not be adjusted.

15. The values of 'f' can be obtained from books and journals. Example: Values of 'f' for tetracycline is 0.6 and trimethoprim is 0.7.

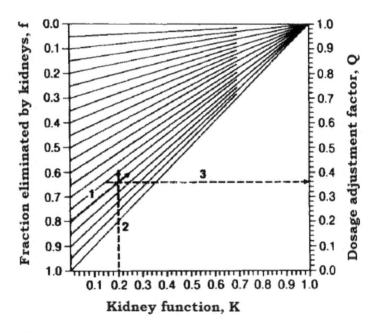

16. If we know f and k, we can calculate Q from the above graph.

5.6: Measurement of Glomerular Filtration rate and creatinine clearance:

1. Several drugs and **endogenous substances** are used as markers to determine the glomerular filtration rate. The renal artery carries the drug to the kidneys. The marker should meet the following criteria.

2. The marker must be **freely filtered** by the kidney.

3. The marker should not be **actively secreted or reabsorbed** in the kidney.

4. The marker should not be metabolized.

5. The marker should not be **bound to plasma proteins**.

6. It should not affect the kidney function and should be **non-toxic**.

7. If GFR is decreased, it indicates that kidney function has decreased.

8. **Inulin** is a polysaccharide and meets the above criteria and is used as a marker for determination of GFR.

9. Use of inulin as a marker is a time consuming procedure and hence is not used for determination of GFR.

10. **Creatinine** is an endogenous substance produced by muscle metabolism in the body. It is a waste product and is filtered by the kidney. It meets all the above criteria and is used for determination of GFR.

11. The creatinine clearance is around 95 ml/min in women and 120 ml/min in men. This value changes with age of patient also.

12. GFR = Creatinine clearance = UCR x V / 1440 x SCR

13. UCR = concentration of creatinine in urine sample.

14. V = volume of urine collected in 24 hours (1440 minutes)

15. SCR = Serum creatinine concentration.

16. Creatinine clearance is ratio of rate of creatinine excretion and plasma concentration of creatinine.

17. The person has to collect the urine for 24 hours. The amount of **creatinineexcreted in 24 hours** is found out.

18. Amount excreted / 1440 minutes, gives the excretion rate of creatinine.

19. Now divide this value by the plasma concentration of creatinine, we will get the creatinine clearance.

20. Example: SCR is 0.012 mg/ ml of blood, UCR is 1 mg/ml, V = 2000 ml / 1440 minutes, calculate GFR.
21. GFR = 1 x 2000 /1440 x 0.012 =115.7 ml/min.

5.7: Creatinine clearance values in special population:

1. The creatinine clearance is around **95 ml/min** in women and **120 ml/min** in men.

2. This normal value is for people having an average body surface area of **1.73 m²** and an average weight of 70 kg.

3. Creatinine clearance values must be considered carefully in **obese**, elderly and emaciated (extremely thin with less muscle mass) patients.

4. In elderly and emaciated persons **muscle mass is less** and they produce less creatinine. However, serum creatinine concentration may be in the normal range because of less renal excretion.

5. In case of obese patients, creatinine clearance should be calculated on **ideal body weight basis.**

6. If creatinine clearance is calculated on **total body weight** (TBW), it will exaggerate the creatinine clearance value.

7. The following equations are used to calculate lean body weight in obese persons.

8. LBW Men = 50 Kgs + 2.3 Kg for each inch over 5 feet.

9. LBW Women = 45.5 kg + 2.3 Kg for each inch over 5 feet.

5.8: Calculation of creatinine clearance from serum concentration only:

1. Problem of collecting 24 hour urine sample in patients is difficult. Hence creatinine clearance is calculated from serum concentration only.

2. Several methods are available for calculating creatinine clearance from serum concentration. The most accurate method uses the **age, height, weight** and gender of the patient.

3. This method should be used only for patient's with intact liver function and no muscle disease like dystrophy or hypertrophy.

4. The below equation is used to calculate creatinine clearance in males.

5. $CL_{CR} = [140 - Age] [Body weight in Kg] / 72 \times serum\ creatinine\ conc.$

6. Serum creatinine concentration should be taken in mg/dl,(mg/100 ml).

7. For females, use 90 % of the obtained clearance value.

8. Use the following formula for children.

9. CL_{CR} = 0.55 x Body length in cm /Serum creatinine concentration.

10. Dosage adjustment is generally done when the renal clearance value is **less than 50 ml/minute**.

11. Various degrees of renal impairment is given in below table.

S.NO	Description	Renal clearance
1	Normal renal function	Greater than 80 ml/min
2	Mild renal impairment	50 – 80 ml/min
3	Moderate renal impairment	30 – 50 ml/min
4	Severe renal impairment	Less than 30 ml/min
5	ESRD (End stage renal disease)	Requires dialysis

Practice problem:

What is the creatinine clearance in 25 years male with a serum concentration of 1 mg/dl.The patient is 5 ft 4 inches, and weighs 104 kg.

The patient is obese and the creatinine clearance should be calculated basing on **lean body weight**.

LBW Men = 50 Kg + 2.3 Kg for each inch over 5 feet.

LBW Women = 45.5 kg + 2.3 Kg for each inch over 5 feet.

LBW = 50 Kg + [2.3 x 4] = 59.2 Kg.

Now use the Cockcroft andGault method for calculating creatinine clearance.

CL_{CR} = [140 – Age] [Body weight in Kg] /72 x serum creatinine conc.

CL_{CR} = [140 – 25] x 59.2 / 72 x 1 = 94.6 ml/min.

5.9: Extracorporeal removal of drugs:

1. In patients with end stage renal disease**(ESRD)** and in patients who have been intoxicated with over dosage of drugs, we have to remove the drug by hemoperfusion, hemofiltration and dialysis. This is called extracorporeal removal of drugs.

2. In these methods the drug and their metabolites are **rapidly removed** without disturbing the electrolyte and fluid balance of the body.

3. **Dialysis** is an artificial process where the drug is removed from blood into dialysis fluid.

4. In peritoneal dialysis, dialysis fluid is sent into the **abdomen**. The **peritoneal membrane** acts as the **dialysis membrane**. It is aroundone to two square meters in adults. The membrane is permeable to solute upto 30,000 Daltons. Around 70 ml/min blood comes into contact with the peritoneum membrane.

5. A **peritoneal catheter** is implanted surgically. Dialysis fluid (2 L) is sent using this catheter. Drug and metabolites leave blood and enter into the dialysis fluid. After 4 to 6 hours, the dialysis fluid containing drug and metabolites is drained out. Again, **fresh dialysis fluid** is sent and the process is repeated.

6. Peritoneal dialysis is a simple process and allows for **self-treatment**. It **does not require a dialysis machine** and can be done at home.

7. Hemodialysis use a dialysis machine and blood is filtered through an **artificial membrane**.

8. In hemodialysis, a shunt is inserted in the arm. **One tube is inserted into the artery and the other into the vein.**

9. Blood leaves the patient, enters the dialysis machine, gets filtered, drug, metabolites, urea and other waste products are removed. Drugs

and other waste materials pass through the dialysis membrane by diffusion mechanism. Then the blood returns to the patient through the vein. **Heparin** is used to prevent clotting of blood in the dialysis machine.

10. Hemodialysis is faster than peritoneal dialysis.

11. Dialysis is required **once every two days** and takes around two to four hours. The factors that affect the removal of drugs by dialysis are given below.

12. Insoluble or fat soluble drugs are **not dialyzed**.

13. **Highly protein bound drugs are not dialyzed**.

   Example: Propranolol is 94 % bound to proteins. Proteins are very large molecules and cannot cross biological membranes.

14. Small drug molecules with less than **500 g/mole** undergo dialysis fast. Example: Vancomycin molecular weight is **1800 g/mole**and dialysis is poor.

15. Drugs having large volume of distribution undergo poor dialysis. Example: **Digoxin Vd is 250 to 300 L** and dialysis is poor. Drugs that

accumulate in tissues instead of blood are not removed by dialysis.

16. Removal of drugs from blood also depends on the type of dialysis machine.

17. **Blood flow rate** (300 to 400 ml/min) to dialysis machine, permeability and surface area of dialysis membrane, nature of dialysis fluid, duration and frequency of dialysis membrane affect the speed of removal of drugs from blood.

18. The term dialyscance (dialysis clearance) is used to express the removal of drug from blood by dialysis machine. It is a term similar to renal clearance and is defined as the amount of blood from which the drug is removed completely by dialysis machine.

19. Dialysance = CL_d = Q (Ca – Cv)/ Ca

20. Q = Speed of blood flow to dialysis machine.

21. Ca = concentration of drug in arterial blood.

22. Cv = concentration of drug in venous blood.

23. Example: The blood flow rate to dialysis machine is350 ml/minute, Ca and Cv are 30 and 12 mcg/ml. Calculate dialyscance. Ans: 210 ml/min.

24. Drugs that are easily removed have high dialyscance values and $t_{1/2}$ will be short.

25. Doses should be adjusted **after dialysis** is complete.

26. Hemoperfusion is passing the patient blood through an adsorbent to remove drugs and the blood is returned to the patient. It is useful in fast removal of drug in case of accidental poisoning and drug overdosage. **Activated charcoal and amberilite resin** are the two materials that are used as adsorbents. The drug should have the affinity for adsorbent. Rate of blood flow, surface area of adsorbent, and affinity of drug for adsorbent affects the rate of removal of drug from the body.

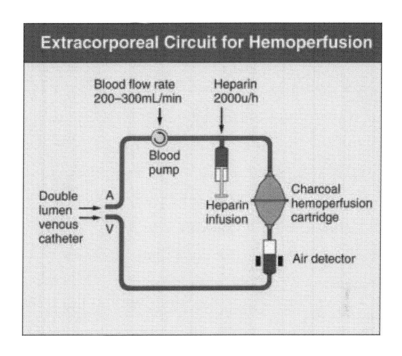

Extracorporeal Circuit for Hemoperfusion

Blood flow rate
200–300mL/min

Heparin
2000u/h

Blood
pump

Double
lumen
venous
catheter

A

V

Heparin
infusion

Charcoal
hemoperfusion
cartridge

Air detector

5.10: Effect of Hepatic disease on pharmacokinetics:

1. Drugs are **metabolized** in liver by enzymes.

2. The metabolism of drugs like chloramphenicol, erythromycin, metronidazole, caffeine, chlordiazepoxide, diazepam, lidocaine, theophylline, propranolol is **significantly decreased** in chronic liver disease.

3. Drug and their metabolites are excreted in bile also.

4. Several physiological and pharmacokinetic factors are to be considered in dosage adjustment in liver disease.

5. Chronic disease or liver damage may alter enzyme production, **detour** of blood circulation, alter albumin, globulin production. As a result protein binding is also affected.

6. Drugs that are eliminated mainly by **renal system** will not be affected by liver disease.

7. Oral bioavailability is increased in liver diseases. This is because,**first pass effect** gets reduced.

8. **Biliary excretion** of drugs gets reduced in liver disease.

9. Drugs having a **wide therapeutic range** are less affected in moderate liver diseases.

10. All liver diseases do not affect the pharmacokinetics of the drug to the same extent.

11. **Therapeutic response** or plasma levels must be monitored and if necessary dose is further reduced.

12. Drugs with **flow dependent clearance** are avoided in patients with liver failure. If necessary, dose is reduced to one tenth of the original dose.

13. Starting the therapy with **low doses** and monitoring response / plasma levels is the best strategy in patients with liver disease.

14. Drug elimination in the body can be divided into fraction excreted unchanged (fe) and fraction metabolized by liver (1- fe).

15. Fraction of drug metabolized = 1-fe = Cl_h / Cl.

16. Cl_h = hepatic clearance, Cl = Total body clearance.

17. Cl_h = Cl (1-fe).

18. The above equation is used to calculate the remaining hepatic function in the patient. It is assumed that metabolism takes place only in liver and the remaining drug is excreted by kidneys.

19. Example: The hepatic clearance of a drug is reduced by 50 % in a patient due to viral disease of the liver. The renal drug Clarence (fe=0.4) and protein binding of drug is not affected. How is the total clearance of drug affected? what should be the dose in the patient?

20. $D_{hepatatis}$/ D_{normal}= Fraction of liver function (1- fe) + fe

21. $D_{hepatatis}$/ D_{normal}= 0.5 (1- fe) + fe

22. $D_{hepatatis}$/ D_{normal}= 0.5 (1- 0.4) + 0.4=0.5 x 0.6 + 0.4
=0.3 + 0.4= 0.7

23. $D_{hepatatis}$= 0.7 x D_{normal}

24. So, the dose should be 70 % of the normal dose.

25. Total clearance of drug is reduced by 30 %.

Hepatic blood flow and clearance:

1. Hepatic blood flow decreases in **viral hepatitis** and chronic alcohol use.

2. This reduces extent of drug metabolism and bioavailability of drug increases.

3. The following equation can be used to calculate the hepatic clearance in the patient.

4. $Cl_h = Q\ Cl_{int}\ /\ (Q + Cl_{int})$

5. Q is quantity of blood flow and Cl_{int} is intrinsic clearance. Ability of the liver enzymes to metabolize the drug is called **intrinsic clearance**.

6. Electromagnetic techniques and ultra sound techniques are required to measure blood flow. These tests may not be readily available, in such cases liver function tests results can be used.

7. **Hormones** also influence the liver metabolism of drugs.

8. In **hyperthyroidism** rate of liver metabolism of many drugs increases. Example: Theophylline, digoxin, propranolol metabolism increases in hyperthyroidism and may decrease in hypothyroidism.

Liver function tests and hepatic metabolism markers:

1. Some useful markers for measuring liver function are discussed below.

2. **AST (Aspartate amino transferase) enzyme and ALT (Alanine amino transferase)** are found in liver and other tissues. Leakage of these enzymes into blood occurs during hepatic disease. By measuring the concentration of these enzymes in blood, we can know the status of liver damage. In acute liver injury, AST/ALT is less than one, in alcoholic hepatitis, **AST/ALT** is greater than 2.

3. Alkaline phosphatase enzyme levels in plasma increase in hepatitis. Marked AP levels, indicates liver tumors or cholestasis.

4. Bilirubin levels in urine increase in **hepatobiliary disease.**

5. Except factor VIII, all coagulation factors are produced by liver. Therefore hepatic disease affects coagulation. Decrease in prothrombin time (rate of conversion of prothrombin to thrombin) indicates acute liver failure.

6. Serum bilirubin is used to assess **biliary obstruction**.

7. Presently there is no single test to know the status of liver functioning or liver disease.

8. A series of tests are done to know the extent of liver function. Example of these tests includes the ability of the liver to eliminate marker drugs such as **Antipyrine, indocyanine green and galactose.**

9. Most liver function tests indicate that whether the liver is damaged or not. It will not give an idea of the functioning of **cytochrome P 450** enzymes which are responsible for metabolism of drugs.

Unit 6: Population Pharmacokinetics

6.1: Introduction to Bayesian theory / Baye's formula / Baye's rule / Baye's probability:

1. Bayesian theory was **originally developed** to improve the diagnosis of a disease by the physician.

2. The physician observes the **symptoms of the patient** and fixes a probability that the patient has a disease. Then he orders laboratory tests. From lab results, he revises his probability.

3. The formula for calculating the revised probability is given below.

$$P(A|B) = \frac{P(B|A)\ P(A)}{P(B)}$$

THE PROBABILITY OF "B" BEING TRUE GIVEN THAT "A" IS TRUE ↓ $P(B|A)$

THE PROBABILITY OF "A" BEING TRUE ↓ $P(A)$

THE PROBABILITY OF "A" BEING TRUE GIVEN THAT "B" IS TRUE ↑ $P(A|B)$

THE PROBABILITY OF "B" BEING TRUE $P(B)$

4. The vertical bar stands for given that.

5. P(A) and P(B) are probability of events A and B and do not affect each other.

6. P(A|B) is conditional probability, probability of event A being true given that event B is true.

7. P(B|A) is the conditional probability, probability of event B being true given that event A is true.

8. Example: The doctor observes the symptoms and fixes the initial probability of having the disease is 60 %. So, the probability of the patient having typhoid is 60/100 = 0.6.

9. So, P(Typhoid disease) =P(A) = 0.6

10. The physician orders for a blood test which is 99 % accurate. It means if 100 patients have typhoid, it will show positive result in 99 patients.

11. So P(Positive test/Typhoid present) = P(B/A) = 0.99

12. Out of 100 blood tests that the doctor sends, 75 are positive and 25 are negative results. P(B) = 75/100 = 0.75

13. P(Typhoid disease) = P(A) = 0.6

14. P(Positive test) = P(B) = 0.75

15. P(Positive test/ Typhoid) = P(B/A) = 0.99

16. P(Typhoid/Positive)= P(A/B)= ?

17. P(A/B) = 0.99 x 0.6 / 0.75 = 0.792

18. Conclusion: There is a 79.2 % chance that the patient has the disease, if the lab result is positive.

6.2: Adaptive method or dosing with feedback:

1. Bayesian theory is used in fixing the **dosage regimen** for a patient.

2. **Priori drug dosing:**First the dose and dosage regimen is fixed for a patient basing on the, population pharmacokinetics, disease condition, age, and weight, sex, and serum creatinine concentration. This is also called **priori kinetics** or population kinetics.

3. Now blood samples are taken and analyzed for dug levels. Now this information is used in Bayesian equation to calculate and fix the new dosage regimen. This method is known as adaptive method or dosing with feedback.

4. Theophylline has a therapeutic window of 10 to 20 mcg/ml. If serum concentration is above 20 mcg/ml, side effects like nausea, insomnia etc. are seen. Above40 mcg/ml, severe side effects like tachycardia, arrhythmia are seen. Some patients have side effects at very low concentrations. The clinician should assess the probability of side effects, order a blood test for theophylline concentration and then calculate a **posterior probability** for side effects in the patient.

5. A nomogram is shown below for calculating the probability of side effects. The initial probability is plotted on x axis and the posterior probability is

plotted on y axis for various serum theophylline concentrations.

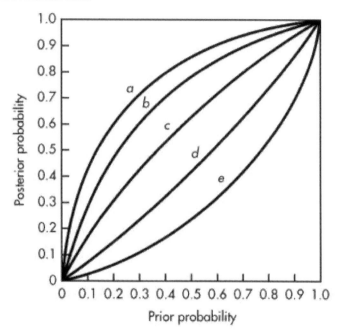

6. For example, a patient was placed on theophylline and the physician estimated a chance of 40 % for side effects, but therapeutic drug monitoring showed a plasma concentration of 27 mcg/ml. A vertical line from prior probability of 0.4 intersects curve 'a' at 0.78. Hence the Bayesian probability of the patient having side effects is 78 % taking into consideration the serum concentration and initial probability of the physician.

7. The curves from a to e are called conditional probability curves for various theophylline concentrations in mcg/ml and ranges are given below.

8. Curve a: Serum theophylline concentration between 27 to 28.9

9. Curve b: Serum theophylline concentration between 23 to 24.9

10. Curve c: Serum theophylline concentration between 19 to 20.9

11. Curve d: Serum theophylline concentration between 15 to 16.9

12. Curve e: Serum theophylline concentration between 11 to 12.9

13. Bayesian method is used for drugs like aminoglycosides, cyclosporine, digoxin, phenytoin, lithium and theophylline.

14. The main disadvantage is the **subjective selection** of prior probability.

6.3: Analysis of Population pharmacokinetic Data:

1. In pharmacokinetic studies, **healthy volunteers** are used to predict the pharmacokinetic parameters of a drug. The average values are calculated and are used to fix the dose and dosage regimen.

2. In reality, the pharmacokinetics of a drug in a patient could be significantly different from that in a healthy volunteer.

3. Hence pharmacokinetics of a drug should be studied in **patient populations** and this information can be used for designing dose and dosage regimen in other patients.

4. Patients are enrolled into the study and whenever possible blood samples are collected.

5. The aim of population pharmacokinetics is to identify and quantify the **source of variability** in drug concentration in the patient population.

6. Population pharmacokinetics is studied in **sub groups** of patient population. Example: Population pharmacokinetics studies are carried in sub groups like, children, geriatrics, smokers, patients with liver failure, patients with renal impairment, etc.

7. The results of population pharmacokinetics will be given in **product leaflet**.

8. Population pharmacokinetics is used to identify differences in efficacy and safety in patient population sub groups.

9. Now graphs are constructed as if all the blood samples were obtained from a single person.

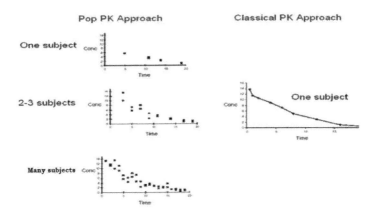

10. From the graphs, the **mean pharmacokinetic parameter** and the **inter subject variability** is measured. This information will be useful to fix the dose and dosage regimen in the sub group population.

11. Example: Pharmacokinetic studies of metformin were carried out in patients with renal impairment. This information was analyzed and dosage regimen was designed for this group of patients. It has been found that it can be used in patients with mild and moderate renal impairment. If GFR is below **35 ml/minute**, metformin should not be used. Up to 2016, it was not used in diabetic patients with renal impairment. This information will be printed on the leaflet for the physician to adjust the doses.

Unit 7: Pharmacogenetics (PGt) or Pharmacogenomics (PGm)

7.1: Introduction: Pharmacogenetics deals with, how genes affect the **response** of a patient to drug therapy. The goal of pharmacogenetics is to design dosage regimen for a patient basing on his **genetic makeup**. This will improve treatment efficacy.

7.2: Genetic polymorphism in Drug metabolism: Cytochrome P-450 Isoenzymes:

1. Cytochrome P 450 is an enzyme that is encoded (controlled) by the CYP2D6 gene.

2. Every biochemical pathway is controlled by a **gene** in the body. The enzyme will work as per the directions of the gene.

3. Cytochrome P450 is one of the most important enzymes involved in the metabolism of drugsin the body. It is responsible for the metabolism and elimination of approximately **25%** of drugs.

4. The amount of enzyme present in the body varies from person to person. If more enzyme is present, metabolism of drugs will be more. In such cases more dose should be given to the patient. These persons are called **rapid metabolizers.**

5. If enzyme content is less, they will be **poor metabolizers**.

6. Dose of a drug is to be adjusted basing on the **speed** it is being metabolized by the cytochrome P 450 enzyme.

7. CYP2D6 enzyme is available in 70 different polymorphs. Out of these 15 polymorphs are inactive.

8. **Poor metabolizers** have the polymorphs which do not have the capacity to metabolize drugs.

9. Generally 10 % of the population are poor metabolizers of drugs. Hence, **CYP2D6 drug candidates** are dropped from further research.

10. Example: Poor metabolizers have increased plasma concentrations of **tricyclic antidepressants** when given in normal doses. Adverse effects are seen and misinterpreted as symptoms of depression and further dose is increased. Hence we have to rule out a poor metabolizer before altering the dose.

11. **Ultra-rapid metabolizers** have fast drug metabolism due to more enzymes or more enzyme activity. As a result, there will be sub therapeutic levels of anti-depressants with normal doses.

12. Pharmacogenetic studies have found that there is some**gene duplication** in some races of people. As a result, they are fast metabolizers of drugs.

13. Around **5 to 20 %** of the studied population was found to be rapid or slow metabolizers of drugs.

7.3: Genetic Polymorphism in Drug Transport:

1. Transporter pharmacogenetics deals with drug **uptake and efflux** into or through tissues.

2. In some persons, there is significant differences in **drug transport** across membranes. This leads to large variations in drug bio-availability.

3. Several membrane **transporter proteins** are available for transport of drugs in intestinal tract, non - intestinal tissues and specific target tissues.

4. Drug efflux is an important cause for **drug resistance** in certain type of cells.

5. Vincristine, vinblastine, douxirubicin, daunorubicin are very good anti-cancer drugs. Some cancer patients do not show response. This is because, they have intrinsic multi drug resistance. They have a

special membrane transport protein. It is called P – glycoprotein multi drug transporter (MDR 1).

6. The MDR 1 is responsible for low concentrations of drugs in some cancer patients. It is responsible for efflux of drug out of the target tissue.

7. MDR 2 and MDR 3 are also responsible for drug distribution in tissues.

7.4: Genetic Polymorphism in Drug Targets:

1. 50 % of drugs act on membrane receptors.

2. The **membrane receptor** is a protein and is encoded (controlled) by genes in the body.

3. These proteins exhibit **polymorphism**. As a result binding of drug with this membrane receptor is altered and drug response is changed.

4. Example: Adrenergic receptor undergoes polymorphism and response to **bronchodilator albuterol** gets reduced.

5. Sulphonyl urea receptor undergoes polymorphism and decreases response to **tolbutamide**.

6. By systematic analysis of genes we can improve drug development.

7.5: Pharmacogenetics and Pharmacokinetics /Pharmacodynamic Considerations:

1. Pharmacokinetic variation in individuals and unexpected pharmacodynamics responses to drugs may be due to **genetic variation** in individuals.

2. The genetic factors affect drug transport, metabolism and drug interaction at receptor site.

3. By applying genetics study to **inter individual variations**, we can improve drug therapy in a patient.

4. The labeling of new drugs now contain information of drug interactions and metabolism based on pharmacogenetics.

5. Population pharmacokinetics study is giving importance to pharmacogenetics also.

6. If a patient is known to be a **non-responder** to a drug due to a genetic variation, we can select another drug.

7. Advances in pharmacogenetics will develop pharmacokinetic and pharmacodynamics studies.

8. **Genetic screening tests** can be carried out in patients to know if he will respond to a drug or not.

9. Genetic diagnostic tests are becoming more affordable now.

10. This information should be used in pharmacokinetics to design a dosage regimen for the patient.

References

1. Applied Biopharmaceutics and Pharmacokinetics by Leon Shargel, Sussana Wu Pong and Andrew B.C. YU.

2. Biopharmaceutics and Clinical Pharmacokinetics by Milo Gibaldi.

3. Clinical Pharmacokinetics Pharmacy Hand Book by Pharmaceutical Services Division, Ministry of Health Malaysia.

Printed in Great Britain
by Amazon